HAIL, CHE!

체 게바라 만세

Hail, Che!

by Pak Jeong-de

Translated by Ed Bok Lee and Eun-Mi Yang

Black Ocean
Boston - Chicago

Black Ocean
P.O. Box 52030
Boston, MA 02205
blackocean.org

Series edited by Jake Levine.
Cover Art and Design by Abby Haddican | abbyhaddican.com
Book Design by Taylor D. Waring | taylordwaring.com

ISBN: 9781965154090
Library of Congress Control Number: 2025945118

This book was published with the support of a publication and translation grant from the Daesan Foundation.

FIRST EDITION

Printed in Canada

CONTENTS

This Poem Is Alive and Flapping

That Is an Object of Mourning

That Is the Wind of Infinity

TRANSLATORS' NOTES

I.

Hail, Che! was published during the Park Geun-hye administration, a time when Han Kang was blacklisted for her novel *Human Acts*, and Pak Jeong-de faced the same fate with this poetry collection. Being blacklisted meant exclusion from all forms of government support, both direct and indirect.

Pak wrote this collection with the conviction that "only poetry can save humanity." The book features over 200 names—poets, writers, musicians, filmmakers, painters—whom Pak considers comrades in the shared mission of elevating humanity through the transformative power of art. He once remarked, "If poetry is regarded as the essence or core of expanded art, I feel a kinship, even a brotherhood, with artists from other fields, such as Jim Jarmusch, Tom Waits, and Viktor Tsoi."

Through scenes of late-night conversations under dim lights, the haze of cigarette smoke, the taste of liquor, and the melodies of music, Pak's poetry evokes moments of deep reflection. His verses summon quiet rebellion and the fading ideals of a bygone era: "Do you remember, Tom? The snow flurries of that time are still blowing here, wetting the window of my room, the light of the factory has been turned off, and the lamplight in the attic is slowly going out, but nobody declares freedom from life anymore."

In this collection, Che Guevara subtly endures as an emblem of international solidarity, embodying the revolutionary force of resistance and striving to resonate with the shared essence of the human spirit. Pak describes this collection as akin to a live performance by an "international poetry radical barbarian band"—a "textual performance" that reimagines the revolutionary spirit. To Pak, revolution is as natural as savoring a morning cigarette, and a revolutionary soul is irresistibly driven to write and perform poetry.

I recall the long summer of 2018 when I first began translating this collection into English. The bright sunlight and lush greenery outside seemed to pulse with life, filling the air with a sense of freedom that felt newly abundant. It was a summer of cautious beginnings and exhilarating discovery.

I owe my deepest gratitude to S. B. Hur, whose boundless inspiration continues to elevate my imperfect words; to Ed Bok Lee, who generously joined me on this meaningful journey; and to Jake Levine and everyone at Black Ocean for their meticulous editing and unwavering dedication. Lastly, on behalf of the poet, I am delighted to invite all of Che Guevara's kindred spirits across the globe to join this performance by the International Poetry Radical Barbarian Band.

—Eun-Mi Yang

II.

Cento of Some Themes in This Book

I've come to the revolution for all

love is a kind of struggle to flare one's own flame

Let's get started, see what happens

Rapture in any dream begins at the point it deviates from the laws of physics

A new dividing line where revolution is born

A poet does things no one else can do

A revolution beneficial to all means we willingly become an outsider to ourselves

If the world doesn't change, what can a poor individual do?

Except to realize one's failure as concretely as possible

Revolution is an animal feeling

Only those who love survive

A boiling midnight revolution

I am a tiny wistful attachment at the far end of that wind, turning dreams into solid things

Today, I call you my music

A cento is a poetic form composed entirely from parts of another poet's or poets' work, in this case Pak Jeong-dae's. As with any poet in ardent dialogue with the cosmos, one can almost at random pull lines from their range of work to create a lucid collage that captures both the blinking, coruscating little microcosms, as well as the larger, darker macrocosms, throbbing within the poet's marrow. One of many energizing aspects of working on these translations was that Pak's poems are also in far-flung conversation with the likes of Lorca, Marina Tsvetaeva, Tom McGrath, Kamau Brathwaite, Zbigniew Herbert, and others, who, each in their own way, document and dramatize a consciousness observing the most numbing systems of their times. In the same breath, Pak's richly ecstatic response to the realities of existence in South Korea, is, at once, furtively affirming and faithful in tone to poetry's oldest ironies. The human soul is untranslatable. Yet, without translation, there can be no gorgeous, ever-evolving civilization, near or far. Gratitude to the Daesan Foundation, *Wasafiri Magazine*, and to the following people, who provided their thoughts on a few especially difficult (or ticklish) phrases: Kjerstin Moody, Jason Ryou, and Ae-hyung Lee. Gratitude also to Eun-Mi Yang, Jake Levine, Carrie Olivia Adams, and everyone else at Black Ocean.

—Ed Bok Lee

This Poem Is Alive and Flapping

TRAIL OF DENIS LAVANT

Today's destination shall be
a power plant in Danginri, on foot

On the way back,
I count the houses of barbarians
scattered like bees on the ground

Shall I go to Jeong's house?
Og's house is too far
Jun-gyu's house is beyond the river like enlightenment

The road to Berlin is boring
so shall I stop by Cocaine for a dark beer?
After Bbang is Gopchang,
but let's get jeongol later

I passed Seogyo Cathedral today
and returned quietly to my attic

And for the ninth and final thing on today's schedule?

A wooden fence beyond walking;
and beyond the wooden fence, in the night sky,
futile tears of only young stars are glittering

REVOLUTION IS AN ANIMAL FEELING

Walking along, I sucked the blood from the Paris plains, giving
birth to its sewers

Each time I sank my teeth into the landscape's passing neck,
peach blossom after peach blossom bloomed, Père
Lachaise Cemetery, Montparnasse, Montmartre

Saint-Lazare station was next to a Chinese restaurant

The Chinese restaurant was next to a little tabac, and the
tabac was next to a peach tree

When the peach blossom bloomed, I started washing the
dishes; when the peach blossom fell, I finished washing the
dishes

Through tens of thousands of blood vessels on the ground, I
infiltrated you

Cigarette smoke is my soul's peach blossom

Revolution is an animal feeling

In the night sky, above the Paris plains, early evening stars,
replete with latent heat, glitter

From the night sky's perspective, Paris was a beautiful
human sewer with stars flowing through

From an ex-angel's perspective, the city of Paris was
invented this way

DIARY OF MOURNING

As light reached a sadness, the rainy season came to an end

In this way life and death are mourned; the rainy season
ended and the diary of mourning began

When a typhoon soars, wriggling its way though, people in
the community of Zandari Uyghur skewer a sheep's
body with a large stick and roast it

Women heat the furnace to bake dough into naan and prepare
herbal tea and walnuts for dinner

The Uyghur people enjoy eating noodles without meat; they
just put a sauce made of herbs onto the noodles,
seasoned only with salt, and eat a simple, light dinner

During Ramadan, they eat dinner around ten, after sunset

When a typhoon soars, wriggling its way through, a Uyghur
family finishes dinner and huddles together on the
carpet, sharing a life that sparkles like starlight

Uyghur beards, sheep beards

As the sheep's life ended, the beard's life began

As a great solitude reached the sloshing sadness, it became
evening

As the solitude of Ramadan begins, someone seated in the
middle of the stormy night sits and drinks his own
religion

It's the way to mourn life and death

As a typhoon soars, wriggling its way through, I sit by the
second-floor window in this building that rattles like
humanity's last train and mumble while watching
the trees shake

As the typhoon gathers on this dark night, let's drink dark
beer

Such a great solitude, now, as the typhoon wriggles its way
through

That is one way to mourn life and death

A bearded angel seated at humankind's final, second-floor
window, is still mumbling

This poem is alive and flapping all night through a typhoon

That is an object of mourning

Over there is Song Gang-ho's goatee

DIARY OF MOURNING

One day, seated at my second-floor window, the night's radical
scenery abruptly appears

The landscape with its deep inner flesh of life is essential and
universal, the radical landscape shows a universal ideal that
people dream of; from here, another diary of mourning
begins

This is a way of mourning love

I sling over my shoulder the green night sky with yellow stars
painted on it and walk the earth's night streets for a long
time

In the ultimate landscape there is always you, and only by
dreaming of you, do I arrive there

On a day when I want to give myself to the breeze fluttering my
white shirt collar, I fly up the stairs to the second floor of
earth and touch down at night at Café Lehmitz

A yearning sprouts, becomes blue leaves, then falls as brown
ones

It's a way of mourning extinction

Somebody lets their hair and beard grow out; somebody ties
up their hair and shaves their beard; but for some the
beard doesn't grow at all

Nevertheless, the night for mourning comes without fail

The night for mourning arrives and cries, showing us the
radical and essential landscape; hearing that cry, I
have a quiet talk with myself

That is a way of mourning love and extinction

The ripe emotion has marched to the entrance of autumn;
when autumn reaches the second floor where the
angel is sitting, the great war of emotion will begin
again

But it's still a quiet night here at Café Lehmitz, the angel
is sitting by the window on the second floor, gazing at
the radical and essential landscape, muttering
something in a grumble

This is an animal way of mourning

That is an object of mourning

Over there are three words of condolence

DIARY OF MOURNING

The sun glowed orange like the eyes of a black goat

As the goat blinked once, a diary of mourning began

This is a way of mourning the desert night

As the goat blinked a few more times, night fell

The night comes like a horizontal black line drawn in the
orange eyes of the goat

Night of the goat with black fur; night, when the sound of
a drum keeps resonating after the skin is taken off and it's
beaten; night of a black ray of mourning

Night, when an angel with an aching back, seated on the second
floor of the old earth, keeps adjusting his posture

As violent heat receded, another violent wind began

The landing of basil by the window; the spindle tree's desert
cactus; the quiet night's speeding

It is a way of mourning the desert nights

Every time the goat blinked, the night became a little deeper

Without an essential affection for humankind, the diary of
mourning keeps being written

Without a fundamental interest in weather, an atmosphere
circulates by itself

Seated by a window of rotating stars, the leaves of my goatee
flutter while the street trees move all night to faraway places

That is a deeper way of mourning the desert night

A way of mourning the atmosphere's fading circulating and the
slowly cooling sun

The angel who smoked all summer seated on the second floor
of the old Earth opens the window a little to send yet
another season out into the distance

This is a whisper of the soul

That is an object of mourning

Over there is the shape of Mother Nature

JEONGSEON, OSLO, GASU-RI

As I wander the evening streets of Oslo, things meet me; if I pass by Oslo's evening lamplights and the houses with pointed roofs, a Viking ship and carriage come into sight; Oslo hides its bars on every street at night—bars like the hearts of its people in their thick clothes; the roofs of this city filled with rain and snow are all pointed like beautiful heels; under those roofs, people are living; this place where so many fjords exist; the fjords appearing after a canyon like a coal-mining region in Gangwon-do, wild nature revealing itself shyly in the presence of humans; Mother Nature is nothing but an extension of the human imagination; people take a ship and tour around the fjords; in the landscape, seagulls fly, and in the sky, clouds pass, although there is difference in scale between them, Gasu-ri in Jeongseon, Gangwon-do, is just as magnificent at Sogne Fjord; the ship is still moving forward, and people who have grown hungry gather for a human evening; Oslo is the Jeongseon of Northern Europe; Sogne Fjord is the Gasu-ri of Norway; when evening falls on Oslo, I go find a bar that is deeply hidden and get a drink; as Norwegian wood is always located at the outskirts of youth, I go to Oslo to smell the scent of an old forest and a river; I go to Gasu-ri in Jeongseon.

LIKE AN ARABIAN HORSE

Like an Arabian horse that smells the desert, my language will
run fiercely towards the horizon

However, at the moment, my language like a weary Arabian
horse has reached a sand dune in the evening; in this
place, there is no my language, no tired Arabian horse, no
evening sand dune

Just like a crazy horse, I'm immersed in the solitude of an old
life, wriggling wildly

Look, a dying horse, emitting a groan; that's my language

Crazy things; things fiercely going crazy

With haste, I ran toward the sun

Ignoring the temperature of the sun, I rushed into the burning
heat like a philosopher with the heart of a volcano jumping
into the world's essence

I ran into your heart, full force, like an Arabian horse forgetting
the smell of the just-arrived wind

Because the scent blowing from the desert inside your heart
drove me crazy

Because it resembled the earth's scent which I used for a pillow
to sleep long ago

I surrendered heroically to your scent

Because I believed your scent would be forever and your body's
heat would complete me

Today, I exit the desert with my head down like a weary Arabian
horse

The temperature of the sun is too hot, the desert drying my
blood

Human emotion is a transmutable material

Looking back, every desert in the world is nothing but a sand
field with the sun scorching it; only now do I fiercely
regret myself, like an Arabian horse that has squandered
everything

In "Like an Arabian Horse," a horse of Bernard-Marie Koltes might be sitting on its haunches somewhere like an animal in solitude.

The horse has probably come from the solitude of a cotton field

Or, perhaps it has come from the night, right before reaching the woods

Anyway, I might have wanted to reach the night of Robert Musil, riding on Koltes's horse

Or, perhaps I might have wanted to reach nowhere, in the evening, on this land which is fiercely, magnificently, perfectly mad; I just murmur, like the lost animal of solitude, like an Arabian horse

SOLITUDE OF EMOTION

In the street, a gentle wind blew

I'd driven from a great distance in a Volvo truck and was leaving
again for another place far away

You stopped briefly at a public phone booth that was connected
to the universe

In your right hand, a pack of Gauloises filter-less cigarettes;
your left thumb and forefinger were touching the cigarette
visibly through the opened pack

The pocket over the left front of your dress shirt was filled with
solitude

Maybe your heart was beating in that pocket

Your neckline, jawline, and the silence of your closed mouth
seen above a thin T-shirt were set against the backdrop of
your face

What were your eyes looking at as they gazed ahead?

With thoughts grown beyond their abundance of hair, I sat
inside the Volvo truck on my way to a distant place and saw
you sitting in the solitude of a cotton field

Beyond the public phone's receiver, the cotton field of solitude spread out into infinity

I was going to a very faraway place beyond comprehension; I might have muttered your name

Your name that was embroidered quietly over the green universe; maybe I muttered it softly

A gentle wind was blowing in the street then

Behind you, a public phone booth was connected to the universe; beyond the phone's receiver, the solitude of a cotton field was spreading out toward infinity

You were there, about to lift a cigarette to your lips

In the solitude of a cotton field
In the solitude of a cotton field

FLEEING ON A HORSE INTO A CITY FARAWAY

I want to go to a snowing Africa, I have to leave because I'm going to die, I want to rummage through trash cans forever, no more words, nothing more to say, teaching words should be stopped, get rid of the schools, make more tombs, one year or a hundred years, eventually it's all the same, that's what makes birds sing, that's what makes birds chirp, Roberto Zucco holds the broken pay phone and leaves with all those words above, there was once a writer who left the story of Zucco for his posthumous work, a story that Zucco killed himself in the same way that he killed his father, I want to go to a snowing Africa too, I want to take off for somewhere because I'm going to die, because I'll be wandering in the arms of Mother Nature forever, so this kind of poem is no longer needed, there is nothing more to say, teaching words and poetry should be stopped, schools should be abolished, churches, nations abolished, the human species should be destroyed, and the world covered with tombs, birds flying over them will spread a new species, this must survive as the sole posthumous work in this world, the solitude of a spacecraft that flies into space and never comes back will arrive here someday, let's call it the sad and beautiful posthumous work of us all, my sad and beautiful one, I forgot your name, to a snowing Africa I want to go

---

Fleeing on a Horse into a City Faraway is the title of a novel by Bernard-Marie Koltes, but, how could I escape far into the city riding on a horse? While I was reading a book by Koltes, who left Roberto Zucco for his posthumous work, I discovered two poems: "Solitude of Emotion," which I found while looking at the photograph of Koltes, and "Fleeing on a Horse into a City Faraway," from a chronological listing of the author. I'm now running away with two live poems, far into the city, but how on Earth can I escape?

In any case, I'm leaving; that's the only way

A GREEN CIRCULATING LINE

This is a green circulating line on the prowl

That is a handful of wolf shining light

Over there is a singular persona

*

For several centuries, the pain has been shining

He already knows the starlight he gazed at with bated breath was a reflection of his own cries ascending to the sky

When animal solitude, wandering beneath the cries of bright memories, gazes up to revive the fading light of its heart, I feel the icy silence of the winter forest on the soles of my feet

As the heart has yet to turn completely off, the earth is cold with pain still shining from several centuries ago

*

I opened night's window and sent more cigarette smoke into the season

I saw moving stars and thought time flies the same way

I listened to the music of stars going back to their hometown

At first, the sound was faint, but, gradually, it became like a magnificent symphony, or a train rattling, or a beating heart

If I ride the green circulating line, maybe I'll come back home

Death was near, but I didn't hold its hand

After coming back home, I opened night's window and sent more cigarette smoke into the season

Like that, all forms of oblivion were scattered into the night sky

DIARY FOR MOURNING

Magnificent sorrow gave birth to me, on an evening when an
eternal wind blew in

A snowstorm whitely pushing forward the winter night gave
birth to me; the snowstorm gave birth to me mid-air before
even touching the ground

I'm the son of a snowstorm, one who wanders the earth on the
wings of eternal wind on winter nights

I'm a mourner in the air; after collecting words floating in
the air, I write a diary for mourning the roofs of people's
houses

On the day when the diary for mourning becomes a warm roof
for humankind, I will touch down to earth with my coat
fluttering, just watch

A snowstorm, a flock of birds flapping their wings heavily
onward to the end of the world

This is a poem of breath not yet touched down

That is an object of mourning

Over there is a body of sorrow still tinged with white light

ATTIC

After waking up late, I open the window, flurries of snow rush in; it's the kind of evening I feel like drinking warm alcohol

Why do I start the day by lighting a cigarette at dusk?

The snow that has blown into the room disappears before I even finish my cigarette. Would countless thoughts drifting upon my mind's abyss disappear like that, leaving no trace?

I switch on the coffee machine and listen to Tom Waits

It's the kind of evening I listen to Tom Waits, leaning the left side of my aching back on a chair

"Godot? Fuck it! I won't wait any longer!"

I chuckle alone, recalling someone's remarks from last night – a kind of barbarian's old habit

"Whatever you bring into the house, I can live on anything. Don't worry even if you can only catch a raccoon or an opossum!"

Now, as your words come to me, it's time to go catch a raccoon
or opossum, blowing cigarette smoke at the world

Outside the window—snow pellets, pellets, and more snow
pellets

To open the door and step outside, this life so vast and deep

ON A LEFTIST EVENING I LISTEN TO TOM WAITS

Leaning the left side of my aching back in this old chair, I listen
to you on this leftist evening

Do you remember, Tom? We drank in some Northern European
port city on a snowy night

In the back alleys of that city, where flurries poured through,
turning into faint piano keys, Tom, you sang a song in a
cold voice that smelled like the wind

Didn't Gypsies rush into that pub?

Gypsy blood flowed in your voice—the wind-like voice of a man
who had drifted on the road for a long time

The night in Northern Europe was so deep and cold that both
singers and listeners seemed like tramps, but who gives a
shit? We were voluntary hermits dreaming up everything
by dreaming up nothing

We roamed anywhere as long as it was outside of life

Another life appeared through a gap in the door of time —Louis Amalek shouted watching a late-night soccer match, and Olivier Durance was staring vacantly out the door, drunk

Life is just that way—staring vacantly, just singing, waiting for things that never come

What is the difference between vagrant and wanderer?

What is the difference between life and aliveness?

We still don't know if it's then or now, but those times left behind will be piled up on the shelf of memories

On that street where death penetrated every moment of life, no matter how late, our friends flocked to the pub

Paolo Grosso, a thug detective, appeared in a black coat; Jean de Par, the Lord of Mustache, arrived flapping his mustache

Everything moving was a poem, and inside of everything unmoving, also a poem

I wonder if you remember, Tom, on that night as the snow flurries drifted ceaselessly like airy lives, that it was you who sang most sorrowfully

On the street of life, where death penetrated, we commemorated the dead by almost drinking ourselves to death

By the time the frozen street was buried in snow, what kind of clue in life were we so keen to seek gathering before Paolo's small flashlight?

Beyond a beer house and a cigarette shop, the light of a factory's night shift was glowing, and, in an attic, someone was struggling to write down the draft of a declaration of life by a light not yet turned off

Is it okay for us to continue to squander away the whole night while somebody is dragging through life so painfully? Just thinking about this scared us, and that fear chilled us, so we sang along to what you sang until daybreak

Do you remember, Tom? The snow flurries of that time are still blowing here, wetting the window of my room, the light of the factory has been turned off, and the lamplight in the attic is slowly going out, but nobody declares freedom from life anymore

A boiling midnight revolution; only the cats are crying

So Tom, sing a song for me as before; the song of a flame
burning sharply, even as swirling snow rushes in

Tom, I'm leaning the left side of my aching back in this old
chair on a leftist evening, listening for your song

THREE-PENNY POEM

If the world feels like a huge public office, as if opening that office's front door to head out into the sun-shining street for a smoke, let's go to Kyrgyzstan

In that place, solitude scatters around like snow flurries

Opening the door leads us to Lake Issyk-Kul, a plaza of water where passionate hearts gather

Let's open the window and listen to the sound of the snow's hoofs falling on the valleys of Kyrgyzstan

The world's wind-driven sources of sound—let's store them up around our outer ears, which are like question marks, and listen to the inner sources of sound that boil little by little like radish-green-doenjang soup being cooked on a winter night

When I try to draw a periodic table for the sources of sound that I've discovered in the world, heart-felt birds flock in and pass in a looping curve, leaving the solitude of a brass bowl of bibimbap

Let's spend a winter mixing and eating solitude

Even in these times when the climate is strange, my cigarette smoke will only play the lute of black nights, and the music will remain as proof that in every human valley where darkness has collapsed and piles up, there were once big snowflakes

A great solitude achieved by silence

A great love that solitude precedes

Let's put life at the forefront of a love that solitude precedes and silence achieves

If, with a flag of cigarette smoke, you establish a nation of coldness and contempt that no one looks at, you will hear the hooves of purity's snow flurries running, covering the night of that nation completely

This is a land of three-penny solitude

A land where new sources of sound are born every day under solitude's star

INTERNATIONAL POETRY: RADICAL BARBARIANS' BAND

Music has a built-in property of going to a prairie's leaves of grass; the prairie is a bed for leaves of grass, their purpose is performance; poetry filled with commas is an interlude of horse hooves galloping to music; above human time, beautiful music like a crow's beak arrives; every poet belongs to the band

Stars shine from every campsite; light harbors the music of imagery within; material exists because the emptiness of air exists; as warmth adopts an image from cold snow flurries, my solitude arrives from starlight shining from far away

I was never there to begin with; the possibility of existing, the maximum effort put into trying to barely exist as a minimum of material; it's the same with sounds—the sound trying to help the existence of material turned into hearing; hearing, coming into hearing, the arrival of sounds is called music

Not every sound can be reduced to letters; meanwhile, all written characters return to sound; at this point, a poem's individuality of sounds is birthed; but here also the limitations and regrets of poetry arise, like writhing insects; they form a band; the poem of a writhing insect raises its voice to give a concert; a performance whose purpose is to become a poem

How can bread with olive oil become a poem and a song? It's a matter of humanity and chemistry, hunger expands images, but expanded images don't reach a warm and beautiful winter; there's no such thing as a warm and beautiful winter, only a musical instrument that plays winter in a warm and beautiful way

Where does the musical instrument come from? It comes from cigarette smoke, coffee, concrete thinking, and wriggling wrist muscles; no, the musical instrument doesn't come from somewhere, it exists everywhere, every being in the world that perceives itself as a musical instrument is already a musically instrumental animal

I write you, I play you, I perform you

It all starts from here

INTERNATIONAL POETRY: RADICAL BARBARIANS' BAND

I was lonely like a substance that has no resistance to anything; in the most admirable corner of the universe, I am occupied with being delicately in solitude; it's not for the purpose of music that exploding meteors are that way; the solitude of a bird that ended its life in the void is frozen midair, that's a star

The boiling water in the kettle is waiting to jump into the coffee; a mixing and synchronicity of things—my faint will help them; I'll mix sunshine, a glass of water, coffee powder, and my thoughts together to make a cup of coffee; a cup of coffee—that's the only music I listen to in the morning

Watering the tree makes water run to the roots; running is embedded with the essential desire to reach somewhere; sunshine rushes to the leaves and pumps water; the empire of a tree-like desire that is quiet and peaceful; quietude and peace depend on intensity and ferocity; I hear the sound of fierce music every time I water the tree

The sound came from a cigarette; from the objects' mixture and my motive; the subtle movements of desire that stimulate the objects; if everything moving is a poem, the sound of everything moving is a live performance of solitude; I smoke a cigarette, which means the smoke I exhale is a live performance by the International Poetry Radical Barbarians' Band

Gainsbourg becomes Gainsbarg sometimes like Fernando Pessoa becomes Alberto Caeiro sometimes; the International Poetry Radical Barbarians' Band is crossing the Pamir Plateau in bright moonlight after passing by a pasture; once they will have crossed the plateau, the barbarians' band will become the Revolutionary Moon Scroll Society

Revolutionary humankind writes poems and performs them

REVOLUTIONARY MOON SCROLL SOCIETY

I have come across the Pamir Plateau overnight

On Courbet's dock, beaks of birds have arrived holding bright sunlight, Courbet's dock resembles a 36-meter-long roll of paper for a typewriter, put together by somebody, a dock of blank white paper stuck together—it's the revolutionary moon, the beginning of the secret society of the scroll

I light up and bite down, standing on Courbet's dock, the cigarette smoke resembles a Polaroid picture; it prints the landscape of my mind immediately

Courbet's dock is thick with cigarette smoke; the origin of the world stems from an unknown fog; from this dense chaos, the wind blows; I don't listen to its songs anymore, I am the origin; wind from new dimensions

The wind's hooves are galloping non-stop; somebody is trying to record the secret history of the world by weaving blades of grass from the meadow, but it's just the history of the world on the surface; the history of the world that penetrates deeper has not yet begun

What comes from a faraway planet, what comes to the road as a ray of brilliant dust, crossing the continent from road to road, broken in the sun, delicately coughing

I listen to the sound of silence, to the great silence spit by the steam organ, Calliope, a great solitude of the world

Monsters unfolded like a roll of paper and disappeared into the Cretaceous and Jurassic periods; the history of monsters vanishing into dust is reproduced in the cigarette smoke I blow; I open the window and release the monsters out into the blue-green earth, a monstrously great solitude

Last night, silences came across the Pamir Plateau

It was Courbet's dock that I reached, horses also coming across, following me; I smoked and exhaled toward the origin of the world; it was a revolutionary moon, the beginning of the society of the scroll

A poem begins like that

A FINAL FAREWELL, TOO BEAUTIFUL AND TOO SOLEMN

On an evening like this, too beautiful and too solemn, I don't want to say a final farewell, so just Tashi Dhele, Tashi Dhele

You are too far or too near, but in the evening, when the wind blows in through the window like now, thinking of you in fear and rapture, I just say Tashi Dhele, Tashi Dhele

Drinking a coffee and lighting a cigarette, I say hello to the early evening stars

Then, Tashi Dhele, Tashi Dhele, twenty-eight angels pass by

Here is Haslla, Siljik, Dowon

"Tashi Dhele" means "How are you?" in Tibetan

I just send my hello—Tashe Dhele—to the night sky of Haslla, Siljik, Dowon today like usual, in a low and quiet voice

Haslla, Siljik, and Dowon are the ancient names of Gangneung, Samcheok, and Jeongseon

High above the triangle of Haslla, Siljik, and Dowon, stars abound, whether then or now

Lunar mansions (28su) means 28 zones, which the Equatorial zone is divided into, based on the moon's cycle of revolution—27 days, 32 days in China; each zone indicates the number of a constellation, also called Seong-su (stars in every constellation); its original meaning: the place where the moon lodges every day

28su are categorized into four parts, with seven constellations, each for convenience, indicating East, West, South, and North, Stars belonging to these four categories are as follows:

East: 7 constellations of Gak, Hang, Jeo, Bang, Sim, Mi, Gi
North: 7 constellations of Du, U, Yeo, Heo, Wi, Sil, Byel
West: 7 constellations of Gyu, Lu, Wi, Myo, Pil, Ja, Sam
South: 7 constellations of Jeong, Gwi, Yu, Seong, Jang, Yik, Jin

Screen International said that it was Bela Tarr's final farewell, all too beautiful and too solemn

On January 3, 1889, in Turin, Nietzsche rushed to a horse that didn't even flinch at the horseman's whipping and sobbed with his arms around the horse's neck

After that, Nietzsche mumbled to his mother, "Mother, I was a fool," which turned out to be his last words; he lived a life in a near vegetative state for ten years before he died

In a countryside village, a horseman, his daughter, and an old horse live together

A violent storm hits outside, and, in the monotonous life they repeat day after day, something begins to gradually change

As I read the synopsis of the film The Turin Horse by Bela Tarr, my eyes pause on his profile

He is lighting up with his left hand, eyes shut, and has a silvery ponytail

Bela Tarr's cigarette smoke wanders around his gently-shut eyes like a soul

I'm thinking of The Turin Horse, while looking at Bela Tarr's cigarette smoke

The Turin Horse shows the road to a storm through silence, or perhaps the road to silence through a storm

Bela Tarr's cigarette smoke is thin and long

I thought of a certain road for a while, looking at his cigarette smoke; the road shows one shape of a soul

"It is Bela Tarr's final farewell, all too beautiful and too solemn," reported *Screen International*

"We don't know what a final farewell that is too beautiful and too solemn even means," answers the International Poetry Radical Barbarians

They just say their hello–Tashi Dhele, Tashi Dhele–gazing at the 28 constellations

THE TURIN HORSE

The Turin Horse is weeping

At the foot of an endlessly stormy hill, the Turin horse weeps
    silently at the world

Riding on the horse from Turin, I pass through a foggy field,
    and the world's landscape is formed anew

The interiors of glass windows look out on the scenery all day
    and weep like storms

A storm is a strong belief, a substance leading to silence

The Turin horse is weeping

Without a sound, the world locked in silence is absent-mindedly
    weeping

That Is an Object of Mourning

LOURMARIN

Let's say, at the central square in Lourmarin,
seated at an outdoor table at Café Gaby,
I drank coffee, polished clouds,
and thought of Marx, then polished Engels
The mistral that blew in last night
took off the ear of a donkey I fed,
an ear of Van Gogh in Arles, as well
I'll add this: Lourmarin is where Albert Camus is buried
I still haven't been to Camus' tomb, and a few clouds
are playing with the daytime moon over Luberon Mountain
Let's say, you are sitting at Café de l'Ormeau in the central
    square
I'm sitting at Café Gaby with my eyes on you
It's the central square
It's just a square located in the center
Let's say, in life, an indifferent exchange of eyes
can become a chance encounter
At the central square in life's bright afternoon,
I polished the following words:
Lourmarin, Marx, Engels,
mistral, donkey, Albert Camus
Let's say, Luberon, Luberon
I haven't yet polished Mount Ventoux in the distance

RENEWAL

Now is the season of the north wind, the mistral just slipping out of the valley of Durance; why is the mistral coming? The indigo sky spreads out over the red roofs studded with birds like black braille; the default of orderly things moving, while dreaming of rehabilitation, I'm the one who is blind to the sun, still gloomy, even amid your full scent of lavender, I stand at this road where the mistral is blowing in; the mistral has come along the river, the Rhone, why does the mistral come? Over the shoulders of the earth, which has stopped rotating, the night arrives like a monk in a black robe, turning off the lit street lamps one by one, a default of orderly things unmoving; a civil war that has started in my heart escalates here into cool starlight on the inner side of Provence; the mistral passes by in an infinite winter; why is the mistral passing yet again? On this night, the great wind passes, licking at life's window like a beast, the hot blood of a heart not infected with love anymore; only a wild shooting star of thoughts is falling coldly to the ground, but still, there is renewal, renewal on a night when the mistral passes, embracing the candlelight of an admirable heart, I whoosh through to renew my past life, even more powerfully

PARDON, PARDON PAK JEONG-DE

Pardon, I have no choice but to say hello first like this

Pardon Les Deux Magots, Sorry, Two Chinese dolls

One day I visited him at his apartment in Paris; he was an ex-angel; it was a season when all the people were on summer holiday; we were supposed to meet at a café below his place; at that time, I was preparing for my seventh book; the following dialogue is what I more or less copied from a conversation with him, the ex-angel.

You once said that people who write poems are all ex-angels, what does it mean?

A poet is already perfect enough, alone with their being, while you're interviewing me, you'll probably ask yourself five or six times, "Oh my god, it's really a wonderful story, but what on earth is he talking about?"

A poet makes a fist and draws a skull on it during an interview; perhaps a poem is what reveals the beauty hidden within the beast, like magic, a poem is an object that is hard to easily explain; now I'm going to explain to you poets and poems with all my effort, but how can you transfer my gestures, my facial expressions, my giggling sounds into print? Writing a poem is very internal and lonely work; in a sense, the image of a poet itself is a poem; while you're interviewing me, you're reading a poem

The most crucial decision in my poetry-writing is made at the final moment when chance plays a very important role; on one hand, I could say I've been writing the same poem repeatedly over and over; in a sense, people are all different, an individual's personality is the result of the childhood one has endured, whether they are conscious or unconscious, they spend their entire lives rehashing the same one idea.

Writing poetry is a great expedition, a poet writes a poem to discover something, purely for personal reasons; it means that writing poetry is a private process through the means of expression called a poem, which should target as small a number of readers as possible; as long as a poem delivers interesting emotions with its own perspectives, nobody will complain about the technical errors; if anybody has an urge to write a poem at this moment, regardless of what you don't know, just jump in, then you'll know; this is the surest and the most fundamental way to do it

To some extent, you can learn from others' poems, but there is a risk of falling into making an homage, after reading a great poet's poem, you can imitate it in your own poems, however, it doesn't work if your imitating is based on just pure respect for the poet; it's only helpful when you find out a solution to your own problems through others' poems, and then its influences can properly apply to your poems; while you think that "borrowing" is just based on the respect for the poet, the true hidden intention behind it is "stealing," and perhaps there is nothing more justified than stealing, if you need it, never hesitate, every poet steals

Thanks to intuition and improvisation, and decisions based on unforeseen accidents, poems get filled with magic

Actually, when I write a poem, I often don't worry about what kind of passage I'm writing, I just keep listening to music, because if I'm a good poet, I'll manage to write good lines correctly without any doubt, therefore as I listen to music well-suited to the mood, I focus more on matching the poem to the music

Whether or not I adopt the music to my poetry, the original music is still there in it, although it's neither visible nor audible, like a ghost; the existence of music makes God come to life and move, and maybe that is poetry

Originality in poetry is an illusion, poetry is not a sacred book, every poet has their limit, when writing poetry, I control nothing

The interviewer who is interviewing me now could be Laurent Tirard, or myself; what I'm saying now could be my words, or the words of others who once granted an interview to Laurent Tirard; the interviewer and interviewee could actually be every person in the world; anyway, what's wrong with that? To borrow a film title by Pedro Almodovar, What Have I Done to Deserve This?

Where do you think you are now?

I asked him again; he was gazing into space; in my empty intestines without any dinner, I could hear the crying sound of a horse, and sometimes the murmur of a stream, he said, lighting up:

Wind blows, The Tuul River looks to fly up into the sky, and embraces the waist of this old nomadic people like an earthworm; reeds and little aquatic plants around Mongolian mountains flutter like a tent; this is Ulaanbaatar

I meet Chinggis Khan's eyes, his slender eyes, like the island Banwoldo, looking at all the Mongolian children having fun, splashing in the Tuul

Persona, I stand by the Tuul, where a wind blows, thinking of the persona of infinite time

Persona, magnolia, melancholia, Mongolia

The wind blows, this is by the Tuul in Ulaanbaatar, the wind blows from the Tuul, the wind passing through the grassland, Xiramuren Caoyuan, to blow inside me; I call that moment a poem; my poem is crossing ploddingly, on a horse, the inner grassland where starlight pours down

Or, it's just a windy evening in Montmartre

Tell me a little about the friends you often see, and when do you feel that you're a poet?

Every poet has a different name, and every poet's name is ultimately one

Even in this moment of interviewing, an angel passes by between you and me, invisible.

Gaston Bachelard, Ghassan Kanafani, Nick Cave, Rashid Nugmanov, Marcel Duchamp, Michel Houellebecq, Bob Dylan, Bob Marley, Baek Seok, Vladimir Vladimirovich Mayakovsky, Viktor Tsoi, Agnès Jaoui, Aktan Abdykalykov, Andy Warhol, Emir Kusturica, Jean-Luc Godard, Georges Perec, Jia Zhangke, Jim Jarmusch, Che Guevara, Karl Marx, Tom Waits, Tristan Tzara, Pascal Quignard, Fernando Pessoa, Françoise Hardy, François Truffaut, and Pierre Reverdy

Maximum pain is accompanied by love; likewise, the best love is followed by pain; they just have different names for the same emotion, or, I'd say every emotion ultimately has only one name

Isidore L. Ducasse, Le comte de Lautréamont, Arthur Rimbaud, Paul Verlaine, Romain Gary, Emile Ajar, Jean Seberg, Jean-Philippe Toussaint, Jean Genet, Jean Cocteau, René Char, Henri-Frédéric Blanc, Patrick Modiano, Marguerite Duras, Honorêde Balzac, Gérard de Nerval, Stéphane Mallarmé, Paul Valéry, Paul Claudel, Serge Gainsbourg, Jane Birkin, Tony Leung Chiu-Wai, Carina Lau Ka Ling, Rainer Maria Rilke, Friedrich Nietzsche, Lou Andreas-Salomé, Frédéric Pajak, Django Reinhardt, and Maxim Gorky

As I said earlier, poem-writing people are all ex-angels; on a day when I wear white shirts, I feel that I'm an ex-angel; on a day when my senses sprout brightly like a kerosene lamp, I descend to human villages for a drink; on a day when it rains all day, I feel the body temperature of humans by the fire; why an ex-angel feels lonely is because he loves somebody; on a day when I miss nobody, I stare blankly at the ivy clung to the wall, watching tears of air flowing along an ivy's stem; I secretly touch my eyes sometimes, into the desert of pupils where tears have dried up, a group of caravans occasionally pass along the horizon; somebody opens the door to come in, and somebody shuts the door to go out behind, on a day when I wear a white shirt, I feel that I'm an ex-angel, lighting up, existing in the air, calm as cigarette smoke

Nikos Kazantzakis, Albert Camus, Samuel Beckett, Jean-Marie Gustave Jean-Marie Gustave Le Clézio, Richard Brautigan, Jorge Luis Borges, Bertolt Brecht, Gabriel García Márquez, Jack Kerouac, William Burroughs, Michelle Tournier, Ágota Kristóf, Christophe Bataille, Eugène Ionesco, Milan Kundera, Italo Calvino, Kurt Vonnegut, Raymond Carver, Mark Chandler, John Cheever, Gen'ichirô Takahashi, Amy Yamada, Murakami Haruki, Ryū Murakami, Lu Xun, Natsume Sōseki, Yukio Mishima, Luis Sepulveda, Franz Kafka, Alain Robbe-Grillet, Pierre Drieu La Rochelle, and Robert Musil

Molière, Jean-Baptiste Poquelin, Laurent Tirard, Romain Duris, Antonin Artaud

Poets light up in a little attic room and cross the gigantic continents

Octavio Paz, César Vallejo, Allen Ginsberg, Ingeborg Bachmann, Forugh Farrokhzad

The wind will take us where we are heading

I feel the breath of the world every time you dream; you and I are already the most sufficient heart of the world

I close my eyes under a black sun, and dream of a sublime, eternal planet.

Guy Debord, Roland Barthes, Gustave Courbet, Richard Long, Sigmund Freud, Carl Jung, Oscar Wilde, Saint-John Perse, Heinrich Boll, Hermann Hesse, Wolfgang Borchert, Edward Said, Theodor Adorno, Georg Wilhelm Friedrich Hegel, Hong Sang-soo, Constantin Brâncu□i, Vincent van Gogh, Paul Gauguin, Dan Flavin, John Lennon, George Harrison, Jim Morrison, Lou Reed, Nam June Paik, Michelle Polnareff, Pascal Bruckner, Miguel de Unamuno, Gus Van Sant, John Cage, John Cassavetes, and Kazimir Malevich

For instance, there are planets like these:

Galsan Tschinag, Osamu Dazai, Maurice Blanchot, Bahman Ghobadi, Bernard-Maire Koltès, Bernard-Henri Lévy, Banksy, Abel Ferrara, Alain Badiou, Judith Hermann, Juli Zeh, Jean de Par, Jean-Luc Nancy, Georges Moustaki, Julia Kristeva, Cesare Pavese, Karel □apek, Tristram Hunt, Ferdinand de Saussure, Peter Handke, Peter Høeg, Francis Wheen, Friedrich Engels, Pierre Paolo Pasolini, Philippe Sollers, Henry David Thoreau, An island made for walking, and Pakjjeong:de

Poems are written for a community that cannot be disclosed

Henri Michaux, Ernst Jandl, Friederike Mayröcker, Ho Chi Minh

Poems are written for a community that cannot be disclosed, and consumed by a community that cannot be disclosed; at the bottom of this secret distribution structure, there lies a solidarity of love and soul that cannot be disclosed

Wisława Szymborska, Ai Qing, Aleksandr Aleksandrovich Blok, Anna Akhmatova, Sergei Yesenin, Boris Pasternak, Yevgeny Yevtushenko, Andrei Voznesensky, Joseph Brodsky, Charles Pierre Baudelaire, Pablo Neruda, Ezra Pound, Thomas Stearns Elliott, Reiner Kunze, Edna St. Vincent Millay, Sylvia Plath, Ted Hughes, Hans Magnus Enzensberger, Francis Ponge, Franz Kafka, Robert Choate Darnton, John Donne, Paul Éluard, Philippe Jaccottet, Jules Supervielle, Jacques Prévert, Susan Sontag, Herbert Marcuse, Johan Huizinga, Yves Bonnefoy, Yordan Yovkov, Aldo Leopold, Isadora Duncan, Edward Hopper, Isabel Miller, Max Picard, Glenn Gould, Virginia Woolf, Christoph Meckel, David Herbert Lawrence, Bernard Miller, Pascal Mercier, Cyrano de Bergerac, Marquis de Sade, Patrick Süskind, Wolf Wondratschek, Arto Paasilinna, Jim Morrison, Wim Wenders, Wong Kar-wai, Li He, Lee San, Henri Bosco, Charles Bukowski, Ibrahim Ferrer, Hugo Ball, Janis Joplin,

Victor Stoichita, Gwenaëlle Aubry, Robert M. Pirsig, Tim Burton, Johnny Depp, Omar Khayyam, Nathalie Sarraute, Rivka Galchen, Cristina Peri Rossi, Federico García Lorca, Théodore Monod, Christine Orban, Roger Grenier, Christian Barosch, Blaise Cendrars, Jean Giono, Roger Nimier, Marguerite Yourcenar, Pascal Jardin, Vincent Delacroix, Woody Allen, David Lynch, Pedro Almodóvar, Emmanuel Levinas, Marie Darrieussecq, William Blake, and Béla Tarr

So-called seditious poems are composed of a revolutionary humor

Isabelle Huppert, Naoko Ogigami, Choi Min-sik, Alberto Giacometti, Jon Lee Anderson, Hirokazu Koreeda, Aziz Nesin, Jean-Michel Basquiat, Keith Haring, Antonio Gaudí, Pablo Neruda, Lee Tae-seok, Leonard Cohen, Malik Bendjelloul, and Sixto Rodriguez

And the poems composed of a revolutionary humor dream of bungee jumping every day at this place—The Pamir District in the Liberation Zone of Revolution City

Garyeong Yuryeongssi (For instance, Mr. Ghost), Gatsan Yagnyeongsi (Gatsan Herbal Market), Godot Amalfi, Searching for Sugarless man, Jinbu Umjikssi (True or False Verb), John Katbek, Paolo Grosso, Grosso Ono, Cezanne

Portu, Provence Che, Lavender Burton, Tim Gwang-seok, Yemikustricha, Guy Cordoba, Clara Marley, Bang Bang Club (Round and Round Fraternity), Munagamja Haruchi (One day's portion of Radish or Potatoes), George Musashino, Gainsbourg Song, Zowie Taste, Solitude Marley, Victor Chara, Tristan Hara, Molier de Amour, Happening Jeung Maan Yuk, ángel Cabaret Voltaire, and Gue Chevara

For instance, living a different life from those above, or dreaming the same dreams—perhaps that is living as a poet

On a day when I wear a white shirt, I write poetry, fluttering my wings

My poem is in the infinite void

In fact, he looked as if repeating to himself, "I have nothing more to say!" as he'd already had several coffees with me; wanting to go back to his apartment to drink his beer, buried in the sofa, in his lonely apartment; perhaps because the time for him to meet an 'angel' was approaching; his mind made the sound of horse hooves wanting to go back to his apartment

Lastly, what is it that you want to say to readers who will be reading this interview?

Pardon Ho Chi Minh, Pardon Pak Jeong-de

The moment I was about to get up, having finished the interview, his face made an expression that seemed to say "I'm sorry;" maybe that's why he asked my name and gave me a poster with his signature on it; it had a long title, "So snow flurries! Cold and hot immortal Buddha on medication, sitting cross-legged, coming to land on this street for now! May you live in these beautiful days!" He asked if I'd like to go for a beer, listening to the crying sound of a horse, the murmur of a stream in my stomach; and I said okay. We stepped out of the café into the street, Saint-Germain-des-Prés, passing Café de Flore, and Les Deux Magots, he took me to Cocaine; Tom Waits' song flowed from the café; by the window, a bearded Emir Kusturica was drinking alone; Tim Burton was sitting by the bar cracking noisy jokes with his girlfriend; when we took our place, he asked me

What will you have?

I replied, looking at him:

The same as you, poet, Pak Jeong-de!

I was actually in the mood for a drink of "in the solitude of the cotton field," but I didn't say that; Tom Waits was singing in low notes with his thick voice; it was night

DIALECT OF BARBARIANS

Here's an old tape recorder

The worn-out tape recorder sings the windy song of a rainy port

Playing the old tape, I can hear the screeching noise of modulation like the sound of waves

I encounter the sound of angel sighs while taking a walk of music; when I move a stone I discover on the trail, the music starts; why?

The wind blows; it's time to go to Ireland

While night falls, a rainstorm rushes in, the roadside trees jettison their leaves, desperately shaking their lives

It's a season I hear about through the magnetic tape recorder

On a night when a typhoon is passing, the roadside trees staggering in the wind, wailing like beasts, I sit by my 2nd floor window, hearing the sound of a garden planted in the night of the world

At a rainy port, blueberries grow

There's a man who wanders around, wearing a cotton field's
solitude

There's an Africa where rain pours, wind blows, and snow
sizzles down

Old night passes through the air, reaches sensitive stars, and
the old tape recorder sheds lonely tears like an elephant

Because there is a star named misanthropy, still today, stars
sparkle far away

Here, as ever, resonates the barbarian dialect

The poetry of a rainy port

**As if getting naked and talking at night, while walking in the
solitude of a cotton field**

I would say:

Human clothes might be the holiest of his belongings

Wandering around the rainy port at night, I wear an overcoat
that fits me perfectly

Words by Koltès are carved in Gothic script as if getting naked
at night

Talking, while taking a walk in the solitude of a cotton field, I would say:

My language will run fiercely toward the horizon like an Arabian horse that has smelled the desert

According to the Barbarian Telegraph magazine, dreams are cliches, so dreams also feel ecstatic

Jinbu Salon is near Monceau Park in the 8th arrondissement in Paris

It's old-fashioned; I like that old style of Jinbu Salon

In the evening, my friends gather at the Jinbu Salon—they're all radical barbarians

We gather there to drink for many days then die, at the same time, slamming our heads on the table at the Jinbu Salon

Like birds fly somewhere to die, radical barbarians come to Jinbu Salon to die

When a gaze drifts around for some time, then finally settles in somewhere, it believes it's in a place, neutral and free

Rapture in any dream begins where it deviates from the laws of physics

In that sense, dreams are something to be explored along with modern physics

A diver who plunges into the deep sea of a dream won't return to reality anymore

The more addictive the dream, the less meaningful reality becomes

A powerful addiction to dreams—I once had such a dream

The reason why I'm here is to fill the abyss of desire, arouse desire, name it, drag it out onto the ground; when shape and weight are given to desire, a cruelty inevitably accompanies it; to give shape and weight to it

People in a picture are moving slightly

As the paused scene in the picture begins to move, the dream also begins

People moving in the picture live in the time zone when the picture was taken

That means the landscape and time captured in the picture maintains a kind of independence from physical reality

Although visible things have the right to decide on the images in a dream to the very end, it is up to the human to decide the content and atmosphere of the dream

For instance, I lie down under a wisteria and have a dream

A dream of climbing the world's pillar, winding to the left, with the polished purple of wisteria blossoms

Something really cruel and terrible is when a person or beast leaves another person or beast in an unfinished state

I go upstream along several valleys like music

Valleys deep with a dense forest that generates a coolness under my feet

Far away, the faint outline of a mountain reveals itself; I'm flying so softly, so freely through the sky

As I pass by mountains, a city comes closer to me

I'll settle down in this city today

While walking the streets of this city, I'll touch its bare skin

Night of an overcoat called angel; night wearing an overcoat

The genitals of an angel sit alone, waiting, lonely, forgetting,
moving from one place to another over time

I dream of sitting blankly in a café, Les Deux Magots

A dream of gazing at the darkening street, returning to my hotel
called Solitude by late evening, dreaming about myself

Sometimes I dream of disappearing, leaving no trace, with a
Parisian whose hips are beautiful

*It's a world of exhausted fighters—memories become a final comfort to
the fighters; memories, the secret weapon that people must carry,
even as they get naked*

The port where dealers of secret weapons traffic their dreams at
night without ever falling asleep is called "Reindeer Star"

The potential of all impossible things

Where the potential of all possible things effervesces like foam

Unidentified memories that transcend all national borders
have been piled up in an old warehouse

The ship has already left the port, while the dream is still
anchored

As the tide ebbs and flow, rolling with the wind, I walk along the breakwater, whispering with the stars

The beach is a recording studio; the seawall is a recorder of waves

Strolling there, I compose a piece of music for you

Then, like a person who runs out of all his memories, I rub my eyes to gaze at the essential landscape of this world—that's when you come to me

Like a secret contact, into the flame of a gaze

When I said, "Hey friend, got a light?" it was not because I wanted to smoke, I just wanted to talk to you, friend

Also, I needed a flame since it had been raining for a long time

While I lay down by the window of damp dreams, I received a visit from raindrops knocking all day long; I dreamed, from morning until night, while listening to the sound of rain

Refusing so stubbornly to be integrated into such a stubborn world, what was it that I dreamed of?

As if nothing happened, I raised my body from its seat, beat the dust off my clothes, and walked out along the raining street

When I stopped walking to say, “Hey friend, got a light?” it was not because I wanted to smoke, I just wanted to talk to you, friend

I wanted to feel the body temperature of the words spoken by others

I wanted to talk to you after forcing myself out of such stubborn silence because you were the sole and holy overcoat of my life

I attempted to seek something like meadows even in this chaos

Yes, I did, even though there are no meadows in this world anymore, I’ll keep wandering through this chaos, searching for a meadow

Even though it’s just a dream, let’s wear each other like warm overcoats, with a gentle stare

Human clothes might be the holiest of all belongings

Don’t say anything, don’t move, I’ll look at you, I love you, friend, I wandered through this chaos searching for someone angelic

And you’re here, I love you, and what’s left with me is beer, beer

I don't know yet how to tell this story, this mess, this rubbish world

Friend, and, always, rain, rain, rain

I didn't mean to say all these sorts of things to you; well, anyway, goodbye

According to the Barbarian Telegraph magazine, sparkling lime Perrier, made in France, is bitter

Like taking a walk in the solitude of a cotton field while talking naked at night

Even though it's still mumbling, here, as ever, is the barbarian dialect

The poetry of a rainy port

Well, anyway, goodbye

CAFÉ HAVANA

If you go to Café Havana, you'll find six musicians playing quizas, quizas, quizas on a stage with red curtains drawn up, and a portrait of Che Guevara hanging on the right-hand wall; there's Rumer at a table made from a rowan tree, and Jean de Par sitting on a chair made from a loquat tree; on the table before the piano; seated alone before a piano, Yol gazes at the stage; an old singer sings about love, though we say we're done with things like love in ancient times; perhaps, perhaps, perhaps our visit to Havana is just for a drink; behind an old singer, Grosso and Louis dance; while dancing, they utter —we're done with things like songs in ancient times; if you go to Café Havana, you'll find a faint gas lamp hanging on the stage's left-hand wall, and Shikoku, high on an anti-addiction medication, sits at the outdoor table, murmuring—I'm done with things like alcohol in ancient times; if you go to Café Havana, you will find a cherry pink mambo, and the café owner, Choi, dozing at the counter from time to time, and Og sitting at table 7 has a drink, muttering—today is the best day of my life; life is too short for dozing; I quit things like sleep a thousand years ago; Café Havana is a place where like-minded souls gather; perhaps our visit to Havana was just for a drink; however, friends of life all gathered there, and, still, an old singer on the stage sings about love, and we say: Things like love, we did it all already

SANTA CLARA

To the question of where he is going,
an old man on a little donkey answers: To Cuba,
then enters a cigar shop

To the question of why he likes Che Guevara,
a young rickshaw operator answers: Revolution,
for all

Revolution, for all!

Walking the World, it's an episode on Cuba
The episode's title is Enchanting Gallop

I try coming up with a different title
Walking into Revolution: Solitude Edition

Santa Clara, where Che Guevara is buried

All the way to this place on foot,
I've come, to the revolution, for all

MAY DAY STROLL

Only people who truly know labor know the importance of
Labor Day!

After asking for the day off at my office, which forces people to
work even on Labor Day, I take a private stroll

I walk around the back gate of Ewha Womans University, where
Labor Day flowers are brightly in full bloom

If the front gate looks like a woman's beautiful pelvis, the back
gate resembles an attractive behind

As I walk through warm sunshine, I could for hours sit and
caress the landscape with my eyes

Even if it's not a countryside porch made of wood, where
freshwater shrimps are boiling over, it's fine

Even if it's not the silvery scales of a river's shimmering waves
breaking on the sandy beach in Pyungsa-ri, Hadong, it's
fine

River of silver, scale-like waves breaking on the sandy beach in
Pyungsa-ri, Hadong, it's fine

My heart is already filled with the light of spring

Shall I go to Susek, where the light of spring and water roll about together?

Shall I go to Moraenae, to see the season of willow trees weeping silvery?

Shall I go to the Temple of the Golden Pavilion in Kyoto, riding on the azure haze of heat, rising list steamy mist?

Shall I pick up that paper cup I left behind on that yellow bus in Kyoto?

Shall I go back to meet that girl riding her bicycle in that alley near Ginkaku-ji Temple?

She must be a beautiful woman now

If I were to meet her again, drinking together all night in a ramen shop behind Kyoto station, how passionately would people curse me behind my back?

I better wear my hair in a ponytail to protect myself

Ah, how I wish I could walk without end on a day like today

I wish I could go missing without a reason

Walking endlessly from Susek to Kyoto, I suddenly realize—I'm a
voluntary patient, a voluntary laborer, a voluntary dreamer

The leaves over there make sounds like bird calls

Quietly, amid the gentle trembling of leaves mid-burn, I walk

Solitude might be there, in the leaves

The bell in a clear spring slowly burning up like reverie

Today I'll take a walk right up to the sound of that bell

WUCHUAN[1]

It's a country where barbarians live

Where two moons and a thousand stars rise,
where wind with only one heart blows

We pour drinks until the one and only sun sets
then drink until a thousand suns rise again

Life is our hobby
Until the hobby becomes beautiful
we pour life into our glasses
and drink the life in our glasses

Love is our habit
Labor is our love
We love like habit, and labor only for our love

It's a place where soulmates gather

NANMAN[2]

A cold rainstorm raged in December
and I suddenly thought of the Nanman
The leaves were about to be scattered here and there by a chilly wind
Namhae or Tongyeong, Gangjin or Haenam,
I suddenly thought of my dear Nanman
What beloved things have been left behind in the south
No matter how hard I tried,
not a single ray of warm sunlight entered my mind
Did a handful of snowflakes boiling in a thin metal pot
one winter evening
become a poor, lonely someone's warm meal?
I suddenly thought of my delicate Nanman
which once faded like fallen leaves
Milky-white snowflakes flew through the air and glittered at an evening lamplight
and I felt a vague sorrow for things scattered away
and pondered the warm unity of things once dispersed, then gathered
Suddenly, I hung my eyes in the air
left behind by a raging December rainstorm
Standing beneath the edge of eaves where the rain fell,
smoking vacantly,
I considered my dear Nanman

UNDER THE INFLUENCE OF SATURN

Today, I labored over music

It took me a month and a half to walk from our northernmost Bukkwan[3] to our southernmost Tongyeong; whenever it rained, the footprints left behind turned into small ponds, and the rims of them formed mounds leading to the wetlands

The ducks went back and forth, as ducks will, while I, too, went back and forth through all of Wangshimni, making my own music of my illness, as autumn steeply descended

In the evening, I had some noodles for my mood of hunger, and gazed up at the starry enlightenment; opening a sealed-up window led to a view of the wind and ducks around Wangshimni, which had fallen fast asleep at the river's hips

When much of the darkness had come and gone, and what remained of night surged quietly, I forgot all about all the reeds and songs of buckthorn and drank together with solitude

In the wind, as the end of a stovepipe like a noodle-maker spun about, creating some monster snake's song, the river simply swallowed its night-long cries, passing under Bukkwan to flow on towards Tongyeong

Today, under the influence of Saturn, I labored over you all day long

EMOTIONAL LABOR

Today I labored over emotions

While exterior walls of the house got soaked in the rain all day, I crouched down in the intestines of the house like a hungry beast, and labored over a handful of sorrows, browsing through the pages of infinite wind

Mr. Elephant, whom I encountered in the world's back alleys was on his way to buy garlic, saying that a vampire was chasing him; the poor Miss Mosquito I encountered during First Frost wandered about like a nomad over the desiccated stream of a desert's skin

Each time this happened, emotions flowed into the sea along with the rainwater, though, as I poured yet another sip of water into the wetlands of my mind, I dwelled upon a newly emergent inner map and its territory

Silence is the pool of water collected in every footstep left by Mr. Elephant's passing tracks

Solitude is a patch of territory that swelled from the place Miss Mosquito occupied

Today, I opened the window, and labored over emotions all day long

Falling raindrops cast like an overcoat over my shoulders, cigarette smoke haunted me all day long

Each time I smoked, particles in the smoke showed me a map to a new territory of emotions like a spacecraft landing on a faraway planet

IT'S OLD HERE, IT'S NEW HERE, IT'S NOT THAT PLACE ANYMORE

It's old here, it's new here, it's not that place anymore

My existence, my breathing place, and my breath generate air waves and permeate your heart

Cats' pupils brighter in the evenings and one-eyed moonlight; my mind has long been blacked out, so I write relying on moonlight and cats' pupils in this old place that feels like a worn-out tent, fluttering badly in the wind; the air here still resembles your breathing

This is the kind of evening I drink spilling a few drops of alcohol onto the battered old table; it's been raining down onto the black asphalt all day long; two light bulbs with wings, two wings sprouting from the sides of the window frames

Thoughts made of a piece of wood; a humidity of thoughts that just can't catch fire during the rainy season

The sound that somebody is cooking life, chop chop chop chop, in life's kitchen

Very old nights don't rely on music, very old nights are not lazy, very old nights are not solitary; very old nights are music itself, laziness itself, solitude itself

Waiting for someone's message that doesn't come is like waiting for a group of merchants to pass while gazing at the desert horizon

Rather than waiting like that, it'd be wiser to grow old quietly on the dark side of sand dunes, enduring the Morse code of glittering stars

I might be able to see an angel flying up over the asphalt if I stay put here

Like a man who has no table is like a man who has no poem, a man who has no soul is like a man who has no angel

In order to resist the solitude connected with things, and the disillusionment caused by solitude, I delete all things related to me and take a fiery sip of liquor on this solitary evening that just keeps getting darker

As long as I don't dream of anything like the soul's redemption it won't be so bad to become worn-out, old, and disappear bit by bit

When your soul dreams of the far place from where the winds blow, I am a tiny wistful attachment at the far end of that wind, turning dreams into solid things, quietly remaining nothing but an honest object, free of disillusionment and fantasy

Afternoon on the tilted Earth, mind of flowing clouds

I observe quietly the movement of objects, watching as they shift themselves into silence and peace

Movement of poetry; when the wind blows and the afternoon shakes, I write to you precariously seated at a rickety table

If I sit here long enough like this, maybe I'll see you fly up over the black asphalt

I WANT TO LIVE ANOTHER LIFE

I kick a ball, dreadlocks flapping
Maybe it was the peak of Bob Marley's life
There's a face that suddenly appears in my mind
What my life would be like
if I'd spent my life with that person
I imagine from time to time
It's amazing that I still live on earth
Many people I knew have already moved on to another planet
Since then, it seems, no news from them
Sometimes over drinks at night alone
people I miss come to mind
I'm talking about those people whom
when I think of Kim Sowol's long-bygone line:
"Shall I say, I miss thee?" I miss
My music started from crying,
isn't that what Bob Marley said?
While my music hasn't started yet,
my crying has already ended, Juliana Abudeba,
I listen to her piano repertoire
I want to live another life
I want to move to another planet rather than stay here
in a life in a strange place where there's nobody I know
A new life in a place where shadows come to an end
I want to kick a ball, dreadlocks flapping

Writing a poem on a yellowish coarse paper notebook bound with springs
I want to live different lives from day to day in a moving tent
A life that begins fluttering once again whenever the wind blows
A life unrelated to gravity,
still fluttering even when the wind doesn't blow
The shadow that followed me
I now quietly leave it here
Just one stone of solitude that I like
will I place in my bag
Yes, on to another life
I won't be able to fly again
Well, regardless,
goodbye

GUITAR WEARING A RED SWEATER

In the beginning, there was nothing; perhaps there was nothing;
on the premise that there was nothing, starlight might have slowly appeared

As a horse of time passed through the starlight, its footprints might have appeared; we called them planets

Crows were carrying starlight from the night sky to the ground; we might have called them music

You weren't called music from the beginning; at first, you were just a part of the light, a soundless landscape

In a world where a soundless landscape formed a shadow, I might have dreamt of you for a long time; it was only millions of years later that you, in my dream, finally emerged as a deep-blue leaf

If times are mingled, they become a solid object; you were the solid crystal created by dreams I dreamed

If times are scattered about, birds fly in the sky as simulacres of the soul

The soul is replicated in this way and flies in the sky of eternity;
and starlight nourished on my shadow in a world full of solitude

Today, I call you my music

I have passed by a long desert dune; I'm passing through the sands of time, to reach your oasis

Though it's just an enormous fantasy, I cross the life-long desert like a caravan, addicted to my own dream

You, my guitar wearing a red sweater, my solitary music

NAJEON JANGRYEOL[4]

Najeon is a field of silk,
sunshine is Jangryeol
On a sunny day, I'll go to Najeon Jangryeol
On a low hill there, I'll plant a mulberry tree
On a steep hillside, I'll grow wild grapes
Waking up late in the morning, I'll wash my ears with the sound of birds
Sitting on the wooden porch, I'll have a late brunch of lettuce-wrapped rice with doenjang soup
Washing dishes along the river, up ahead, where the fragrance of grass flowers fills the air,
I might catch morning sneaking away
Longing for a faraway place,
if I bury it in my heart like wild ginseng,
focus on growing my solitude there,
birds will bite sunshine, disappear into sunset,
only to return, carrying twilight
to permeate the shadows of white birch
Najeon is a field of silk,
Solitude is Jangryeol
On a day when the wind blows quietly, I'll go to Najeon Jangryeol
Over there, firewood lit by my younger days wanes;

upon the snow that remains, a night of shining moonlight arrives
If I light up the night with scarlet charcoal lingering in the furnace,
even a love that held its breath will finally glow
A night of belated love will come as blossoming shadows, shimmering in the earthen-cut window
My heart will deepen like mountain grapes
The river will musically flow through the night
On a night when the moon casts shining solitude through its threshold,
my life will still be a lonely beast
I'll love you bit by bit as if dreaming
Najeon is a field of silk,
you are the Jangryeol of life
On a day and night of life when brightly I dream of you
Let's trot on a donkey
into a field of silk in Jangryeol

POETRY

Nothing has a true nature

There is a species whose true nature comes to the surface only when it loves; the language it whispers is close to poetry

*

Today, a few leaves are turning yellowish—they are radical barbarians

Today, treading upon a few falling leaves, a lone bird is crossing the void; that's the singular soul of a barbarian

*

Poetry, a bird wearing a black sweater

ONLY THOSE WHO LOVE SURVIVE

It's a night when a reindeer herd is passing in the distance

A reindeer is humankind's oldest poem, a very long poem still in progress, moving slowly

Beneath a green sun, a reindeer listens to the music; he composes music for a reindeer, so I have no choice but to say thank you, Pak Jeong-de

It was on a winter day that I met him; I asked only one question; as he spoke I changed it to a question

You said only those who love survive; what do you mean?

The following is his response as published in, *Barbarian Telegraph, Crystallization of Voice*; I listen quietly to his music

Only those who love survive

Literally, what that means, apart from the object and temporality: if a soul exists, what makes the "if" possible is love

I know little about what love is; the only reason I, an ex-angel, tried to become a human was because of love; however, I still don't know what love is; insatiable human greed ruined the impetus of my desire to become a human

However, I haven't yet stopped seeking love; No, these are not the proper words; strictly speaking, it's not a seeking, but an exploration into a sole individual who transcends the whole and the infinite

For the love I dream of, I want to actively improve this world; I want to change this world into a place that is best optimized for love; but my dream seems too far away, its possibility very slim

I attempted to love because I want to become a human; No, this is also poorly expressed; I attempted to become a human because I want to love, but every attempt has been a failure

I haven't yet set my feet on the ground, still floating in the air; however, on a day when I want to become a human, I borrow the overcoat of an angel, and write a poem

I only see the hope and future of humankind through poetry

I'm going to try to speak a poem

All night long, a poem wearing red passes the twelve seasons of the heart, walking quietly into a black forest

I'm going to try to speak a poem

Poetry is snow falling throughout the night; footprints walking on a virgin snowfield; a wind sneering at the world; the window of morning; a flag of cigarette smoke rising towards the world for the first time

I'm going to try to speak a poem

From daylight until evening, I was drinking at a tavern called Sherlock Holmes

I remember a white dwarf, and the white night of Amsterdam; I remember the white night spreading out of the window during short smoke breaks while I was in transit at the airport

I remember the sun's rousing cheers passing over the Gobi Desert, and the strange evening landscape when the sun didn't set

I remember the sentiment of such an evening when I felt an urge to seek out any tavern; I remember the bright night at ten p.m. in Amsterdam

I'm going to try to speak a poem

Why do I look into their lives again?

There must be a clear reason for every act, so in the depths of this chaotic city built by human egoistic desire, I reminisce about the communist in a frock coat, and a bearded sage who was formulating his rage into a clear and solid theory while he frequented the taverns in Trier

They knew earlier than anybody there was a pain, and the pain came from outside, not from within

If the world doesn't change, what can a poor individual do?

Aside from struggling with extreme difficulty to revolutionize and improve the world, there would be nothing for an individual to do, except to realize one's failure as concretely as possible

I'm going to try to speak a poem

A society where cigarette-making workers can't freely smoke is not right; what I mean, regardless of right or wrong, something is amiss

The root cause of this wrong is obvious, yet why don't people express anger and resist?

I'm going to try to speak a poem

If they remain neutral, suppressing their natural resentment and resistance, it means that they've already lost their essential humanity

Reading the lives of Engels and Marx, who barhopped all over Trier, I look at myself

The falsehood of the word, *future*; the incomprehensibility of the word, *present*; misuse of the word, *past*; all time is neither passing nor approaching, it just gets mixed together

I look at my soul's comrades in a corner of mixed-time

They are my life

I'm going to try to speak a poem

The night is beautiful; soccer at night is sad; the conversation of wriggling bodies; soccer is sad when it's spread out like a musical score of flesh

Sad like a manager at the Hotel Jarvis in London; sad like the cabbie in a Mercedes Benz in London

Emptiness of the stadium that endures pain; futility of muscles driving a ball; regardless, humans racing towards futility are beautiful

Yet the body is sad when still it gasps while fluttering the flag
of its soul

Soccer is one book; like all the books in the world, there is no
relative and absolute soccer guidebook in the world

If you follow perfectly the guidebook, soccer is still sad

Rather, if you watch soccer while drinking cold beers, it's going
to be a beautiful life

Life is a sad stadium produced by emptiness; grass is green; yet
even that greenness is artificial; yet where on Earth is a love
that is not artificial?

Arthur Conan Doyle wrote a beautiful detective novel, but the
sky of capitalism that steals and sells beauty is still blue

Under the sky of capitalism, where every written word is gnawed
at and grown, poets must resist everything, even themselves

Otherwise, a poet whose heart was gnawed away would float
into the sky of capitalism like a ghost, and eventually
vanish like smoke

Why does drinking San Miguel make me keep thinking of
London's Water Bay and Indian-style bars?

Why do I think of that quiet yet busy bar at the Hotel Jarvis
after midnight in London?

Irreversible time is still circulating, so we don't need to go back
to those times

As time is already returning to the place I eagerly dream of
staying, the night is beautiful, and the night's soccer match
is still sad

I'm going to try to speak a poem

What would be beauty's ultimate dish? I ponder my final recipe

I'm going to try to speak a poem

The night fell like a cat with twinkling eyes; I lit up the lamp of
my heart and loved the cat

Why did the cat that had once talked to me with extraterrestrial
words suddenly disappear one day?

If a cat is love, the night would be a manifestation of love;
without any purpose or future, I just love the black cat

I'm going to try to speak a poem

There is a public place for stray cats; a public place for those who do and do not like cats; if a cat is love, is there such a place for love?

Humans are inexplicable animals, complex and subtle; could there be a kind of common zone for humans to exist? No, it's nearly impossible

If a common cat zone for stray cats is a common zone for love, and it can be well-maintained, it's possible for complicated human beings to have their own common zone in the future

I'm going to try to speak a poem

I woke up in the morning, watered plants, washed my face, and sat at the table

Today's music starts with "Sunday Morning" by The Velvet Underground

The voice of Lou Reed, the lilting sounds, feeling relaxed, is really pleasing; what's the title of the second song? I barely remember

Where would these sounds and simple rhythms take me? How far? I turn down the volume and look out the window

The season neither flows away nor draws near, but just stays put

Running low on Bohem Cigar No. 6s, I smoke a Marlboro Red instead, which causes more phlegm to come out; nonetheless, I occasionally feel an urge to smoke Marlboros; now the third song starts to play; I don't remember its title either; I just listen

Do I really need to know the song titles? Some birds express life through their cries all day long; there's definitely life inside those cries; maybe that life will one day be appreciated in its full delicacy by someone's hearing, therein completing it

Finally, "The Venus in Furs" comes on; I like this song as it feels different depending on the situation; I also like the screeching of something like an Indian musical instrument at times in the background

Listening to this song makes me want to fall asleep for a thousand years

Suddenly, as if everything slips out of life, fatigue sometimes rushes in

I might as well take a rest for a moment and smoke a cigarette

Serblin, I too want to take a rest right now

I'm going to try to speak a poem

The fierce and intense soccer season was over, and now, the wind, reminiscent of rest, blows

I was fierce but not in agony; I was intense but not with the heart of goodwill

However, I won't regret it; life has always been hot enough to be fierce and intense; life accompanied by regret already deviates from life

I drift into a languid reverie, holding pain that is bound to follow when everything is over

At some point, the reverie will be over as well; then I'll quietly fall asleep; in the season of a cold heart, I'll fall asleep with no more reverie or dreams, only the thinnest blanket

I'm going to try to speak a poem

I wake up in the morning, watch soccer broadcasts, and drink coffee, while smoking a cigarette; soccer is a movement from *Missa Solemnis*; a cigarette is a revolution of creaturely writhing and heat

Where is it that I'm now sitting?

It's every place in the world

It's every morning in the world, a journey to the deepest down inside office, smoking a cigarette

I think of the fluidity of a stationary place

In fact, places are always moving in subtle and delicate ways; it's not just a byproduct of psychological headbanging; every place possesses a distinct fluidity

The story about a cigarette that I'm going to tell you now is perhaps about the distinct fluidity of apparently stationary places

Within Kent Boosts, you can hear a horse's hooves that once galloped along the prairies of Hungary; it has a scent of mint

Parliaments are something you should smoke after climbing the Himalayas; you'll know why when you smoke them

On the mountain ridge where solitude has been delicately driven, footprints sing a little song for the wind, left there like composed music

Somewhere, a firewood stove will be flaming warm

On a day like this, you should light a match and watch soccer matches in the rain

On the field, sparks are leaping around, not yet wet; the rain will keep coming down

Che, let's save it, to smoke later

I attempt to write a short book of ten thousand pages in ten days, with an effort to fill one hundred pages of the manuscript paper every day

A very short and beautiful book about cigarettes; perhaps it will become the most beautiful book in my life

I'm going to try to speak a poem

A book about cigarettes; I'll write it; you, my dear, declare it

"I want the flame of freedom; the essence of revolution is to smoke a cigarette freely; so let's occupy all the cigarette warehouses in the world!"

I'm not going to try to speak about poetry

I'm going to try to speak a poem

I eat dried herring made in Guryongpo, I eat braised oysters

Snow is falling without end outside the window; this is a quiet
barbarians' beach where ebb and flow radically intersect

It's a barbarians' meeting on a snowy day

A secret envoy from afar brought a carton of cigarettes; a carton
of secret orders that hold the inner side of countless sparks

It stopped snowing; it's raining; it stopped raining; the matches
at the beach continue

I'm going to try to speak a poem

The answers are a volume of fresh literature; I dream of the
ultimate talk literature

At this midday hour, I'm already drowsy; can I really write a
manuscript of a hundred pages a day? I wonder, and that
curiosity makes me give it a try, with blinking eyes

According to the calendar of Mayans, the year that indicates
the end of mankind has already passed; I just write down
this fact, calmly smoking a cigarette

Even if humankind managed to survive despite the Mayan calendar, it will perish someday; it's the truth

I'm going to try to speak a poem

For nearly ten days, I haven't written a line and have only watched soccer matches on TV

Soccer is surely a piece of solemn music; humankind knows it, which is why it has the potential to become truly great

Even salmon dribble out life with their entire bodies

A night's soccer match is very charming; a soccer match on a winter night is beyond description

However you say it, soccer is soccer, and a cigarette is a cigarette

I know little about why; not knowing is part of my essence

A poem came to mind, no, to be more accurate, it's not a poem that occurred to me, but a poetic sentiment that surged up from somewhere private within

I'm going to try to speak a poem

The unmanned stand selling apples was beside the national highway; I bought a bag of apples for three dollars and enjoyed their sweet juice as a substitute for water; in November, the southern hemisphere is warmer than the northern; in the southern hemisphere, the Christmas season is coming around and dolphins are cheerful; in a seal's natural habitat, seals were living; the unmanned stand selling apples was beside the national highway; I bought a bag of apples and ate them on my journey; I bought a bag of apples and ate them on my journey; from deep within, words of apple-logy were surging forth; I wanted to apple-ogize, but people I needed apple-ogize to were too far away; somewhere close to Antarctica, I was standing at the end of an island, Tasmania, after passing by the unmanned stand selling apples

I'm going to try to speak a poem

I drink coffee; coffee is a creaturely poem; cigarettes are thousands of animal stars; soccer is tens of thousands of music scores

It's dawn on earth

I once dropped into Frankfurt Airport and smoked there; I was on my way to London

Every piece of my writing mentions cigarettes; people ask me
"Why all this talk about cigarettes in your work?"

I don't answer; I just smoke a cigarette

I'm going to try to speak a poem

I play Tango music and watch the soccer broadcast with the
volume down; it's dawn when I try to think of the place
for everything

Music by Piazzolla unexpectedly goes well with soccer; not
unexpectedly; they're destined to be together

I drink a glass of water and smoke two cigarettes

It's dawn when I try to contemplate things I could do to get
along with humans

These are days that I want to live a life without psychological
hunger, by loving someone, making a very private and
beautiful film, and watching soccer matches together

It's dawn when I wake up with sympathy, and contemplate
humans; dawn when solitude spreads like ripening
cigarette smoke

I don't wish for Voyager 1 to return; I wish for Voyager 1 to expand us; vain hopes ruined humankind

I'm alone, but I don't shout out that I'm alone; every human is alone

It's dawn when I listen to the music of Piazzolla while watching soccer matches; it's supposed to feel Pia-hella lonely

I'm going to try to speak a poem

Crystallization of some name, some voice, emerging at dawn

I'm going to try to speak a poem

Through gaps in dark clouds, glimpses of blue sky appear; I drink from midday at a tavern called Sherlock Holmes

In a nomadic life, how could anyone endure without drinking?

It's been ages since I've heard from old comrades; I drink in the daytime, quietly drifting clouds my only company

The grassland of a mind that hasn't yet been invaded is so blue-green that horses neigh whisking their tails; by those blue-green sounds, I get drunk

Love, don't look for me

In the Sherlock Holmes tavern, where even Sherlock Holmes can't be found, I buried my longing for you deep in my heart like stolen goods; not even through rumors will you ever find me

Love, once again, don't look for me

A season, binge drunk, swaying off on a blue-green horse

I'm going to try to speak a poem

No, it's not that I'm going to try to speak a poem

Crystallization of voice; I record a poem

On the last night of humankind, when I write a diary of mourning, I collect the crystallization of the voice that he left behind, to play it for reindeer

On this night of reindeer, when only pure things are recorded, only those who love survive

So I have no choice but to say once again—Pardon; Pardon; Pak Jeong-de

Wow, pow, goodbye

That Is the Wind of Infinity

☆

Ernesto, My Friend

The unbearable loneliness of being makes me write this poem

In the morning, I unscrew a spoonful of soul and drink my coffee; that might be my way of mourning; a resolute ceremony to start the day well

When smoking in a corner attic on Earth, I'm shut off from the season of the world

Inside this closed-off season, I open the window a bit and quietly read the weather of the world

A sentence of solitude, if there is such a sentence, should come here right now to be written

I am solitude completed from the beginning, therefore I flow out from the heart of the world into the heart of another world, while writing a letter of silence to you

Ernesto, my friend

I can hardly associate with anything in the world, so I'm death-defyingly lonely

I gaze at the road solitude has paved; at the horizon, it has widened; I open the window to gaze at the landscape of tomorrow

I'm an angel of descent, a raindrop falling in a straight line between distant sky and the horizon

But now my poem wears the pants of clouds and wanders through the void

Ernesto, though you marched straight into the heart of this world, carrying a gun, I have nothing to carry in my hand anymore

Now, the only weapon I can carry in my hand is futility; a solid solitude grasping futility

I grasp the futility and become heat to infiltrate the insides of the world

Ernesto, my friend

Every morning, I smoke a cigarette that came from the land of revolution

The cigarette smoke I blow—I wish it were a flag that would shake the world, and awaken sleeping souls

I wish I could shake the rotting landscape of capitalism spread out before my eyes, and slap the back of its flatterers' parasitic heads

Many people die every day without so much as a groan, stuck in the laws established by those flatterers

It'd be nice if they could finally sigh

People here have long forgotten about freedom

People here have long set a way of life based solely on the instinct for survival

I witness a huge silence shifting into a bitter fury as if it were grains of instant coffee melting in water

I know that someday they'll boil over and explode to turn the world into the color of coffee water

I know that the cigarette smoke I blow every morning will turn into somebody's flag to flutter all around the world

So, today, as usual, I blow into the void the bellows of futility

The solitude of the world helps futility assemble leaves in the plaza

Ernesto, my friend

The only commander leading me now is coffee and cigarettes; even in trivial remarks and jokes, this world tries to read the commander's face

Thanks to coffee and cigarettes, I dream of revolution every morning

Now I write a poem for the human race—it's the hour of the angel

Today, as usual, I borrow the overcoat of an angel to write this poem

I grow a coffee tree and tend to tobacco fields by myself

The coffee I drink and the cigarettes I smoke come from there

That is my revolution

Infinite freedom infused with a longing for something, and the new world dreamt of by that freedom, exist at the opposite end of our self-centeredness

All sorts of tramps who wander the world; spaceships that can't return to inner Earth; people who have given up on life

The sole force that gathers them together comes from a massive heart of goodwill

The wiggling of a delicate yet intense will, a will to improve the world, already exists in a flutter of wind

To decipher the wind's will with one's desperate mind—that requires the overcoat of an angel

Ernesto, my friend

I eat only one meal a day

It's not because of a food shortage, but because, with only one meal a day, humans can still dream

Friend, as someone once said, humans descend from the world of dreams

However, after descending from one world of dreams, humankind has not yet settled into another world of dreams

Therefore, I'm now trying to speak of another world of dreams by borrowing your name

From a prison of words spit out by humans, from a cruel prison embedded within human languages, let's liberate the breath

A new world, starting in the land of solitude, dreams of a vast land of freedom

Let's have it dream of a factory

Let's have the hands of citizens hold a dream, not a gun

Let's have loving emotion cover up the earth like an uncontrollable flood

Ernesto, my friend

In a corner attic on Earth, I smoke a cigarette and attempt to expand your heart of goodwill

Let's return the sun and the wind to every heart that goes to work at a factory, a company, a school, on the street

Let's restore the heart of nature, and provide it with fresh air

In autumn, ginkgo leaves attend a yellowish picnic; birds discharge themselves of their tiring duty in the air and descend to the ground to take a rest

Let's release just one fresh word like a single horse from humanity's corrupt mouth to go galloping across the virgin prairie

Let's have that word gallop across the earth of humans, as if it were the very first horse in human history

On rainy days, let's embrace the rain like thirsty trees; on snowy days, let's shake hands with the falling snowflakes, listening in on the news of distant snowflakes

Ernesto, my friend

I take off stiff shoes and change into running shoes

Like a sheet from a secret map that would guide me to a new world, the morning breeze spreads out towards the infinite

The roadside trees go on walking into the season, smiling

From the very beginning, this was humankind's Mother Earth

To the very end, it should remain Mother Earth of humankind

Now solitude cooperates with the world and reticence helps it

I move my body and play music to an inner side of humanity

I wear the overcoat of an angel, write a poem, and breathe into the body of the human race

Ernesto, my friend

From dreams we dream together, from companionship we share together, a new land is sprouting forth

That is humanity's hometown

The wind of infinity blows

Infinity's love is shaking me

JEONGSEON

Guy Debord is living somewhere as a gypsy (Wouldn't that be
nice?)
Emir Kusturica is in between Zagreb and Sarajevo
Jim Jarmusch is at the snow-covered Cocaine beyond any
weather forecast
Cocaine is a dot-like island between a blizzard and the void

Django Reinhardt is hanging on a clothesline
Nick Cave is in the cave of Berlin
Gasu-ri is in Jeongseon, Gangwon-do, where it's snowing
Jeongseon is on the inner side of the world between the Pacific
Ocean and the Korean peninsula

South of Gasu-ri, there she is
North of her, there I am

I'm perched on a bridge's railing in Bukdae village, Gasu-ri
It's a live performance of solitude I'm sending to my comrades
of the soul
Here is Radio Rebelde[5]—Hail, Che Guevara

BUKDAE IN WINTER

Bukdae, I think of a different, possible world

Bukdae, opening the window and gazing out as the snow falls,
I think of the possibility of the impossible and the infinity
of all possibilities

The beginning of a road; the road begins somewhere; I once
believed wherever my shoes headed was the road; now I
know every road begins with an expansion of eyes

As the eyes extended outward and touched the landscape,
the landscape revealed a map for a new planet; as you
investigate such a map, you begin to build another empire
of the soul within

Snowing Bukdae; a snowing even in time past when I didn't
believe in love

A meeting of blazing flames and snow flurries; an afternoon in
a cold northern hemisphere where heat embraces heat; I
think of the infinite future of possibilities

Birds wearing sweaters fly away; indeed it's winter

The candle in a heart will burn all night once again

Repetition; thoughts recurring; an extinguishment of the earth is like that of a single candle; build a life upon your heart and welcome a new planet that dazzles like a flame

Getting through winter by a warm stove is what most people dream of; but many don't have a stove; even more don't have winter

Bukdae, where snow falls and wind blows; still the heart of capitalism whispers the situation is catastrophic, but not yet serious; when I turn my eyes to look out the window for a moment, I find everything serious, and the situation catastrophic

Bukdae, where snow falls, wind blows, and it's cold, though what is most important starts with a flame in the heart

As the spark of revolution begins with a stove cultivated by a heart of goodwill, the people's hearts craving bread, wine, and freedom have always been the initial kindling

When snow flurries scatter in the evening, I ignite solitude with a match and gaze at the distant starlight

As I quietly chew loneliness, somebody breaks the silence to enter it, but I don't have any loneliness left to share; a finite loneliness; a loneliness of fixed quantity

I write words that nobody cares about, and insist they should be a poem—that is my poetry

The sound of the wind blowing from somewhere and passing me by—that is my music

Don't rush me, I have nothing to give you

Try again, fail again, fail better

Someone is a member of the International Poetry Radical Barbarians' Band, while others are in a band named Mrs. Sa's Dissipated Life

If Kim Soo-young was still alive, he would organize a band called Delirious Apricot Stone Band

However, from here on out, I'll traverse the long, inner road with only solitude; every revolution wears its own sweater

Light ignites the flame

Therefore, love is a kind of struggle to flare one's own flame

It's very sad that a revolution for human dignity can only succeed when the opposition possesses at least a minimum of ethics

Now I'm looking at a landscape that doesn't permeate music; somebody is playing the music that doesn't permeate the landscape; the world is only a world within its own spectrum

A revolution beneficial to all means; we willingly become an outsider to ourselves

Pick a place, write, and add music to it; that's how my poetry becomes complete

No need to make a big fuss, as if a poet is doing something great; however, what a poet has done might be something greater than what a non-poet has done in their lifetime; a poet does things no one else can do

Bukdae, where snow falls, wind blows, and windows rattle; a well-meaning heart in a sweater is thinking of the theme of revolution

Being prepared to fight against all that oppresses humanity, resolutely, I light a cigarette

All the cigarette smoke in the world exists in resolute support of an accurate judgment of where pain gets created amid the unconscious human desire to eliminate that pain

When light ignites a flame, another light creates objects

Snowflakes from afar are washing the old, worn-out window

Bukdae, let's close our eyes and gaze out upon a secret, beautiful
landscape

Light creates objects

Through the pouring snow, a tree stands in the middle of
Bukdae; only the trunk is visible; its branches and leaves
extend infinitely beyond all snow

A new dividing line where revolution is born; that is a kind of
symbol

GAZER

Some days are magnificent from morning on

Let's proceed through the mirror and explore the illusion

Let's get started, see what happens

What is worth doing at least once and what will never stop is worth repeating over and over

Life is too important to be considered dead serious

Even if the poem I write is terrible, it's in my own way that I write it terribly

On a snowy day, I write a poem looking out the window; poetry carries a shipwreck and a gene for disappearance; when stars with keen senses sail through space depending on the weather chart of sound, my solitude plays stellar music; on a snowy day, I cross the infinite, looking out the window

Poetry is the sole allied force of the poet, the root of their power, upon which all determinations are based, however arbitrary

A glass of spirits gives initial clues to a poem to begin drawing its own conclusions; drinking together with you is poetry's sole ally

There are pupils inside your lips, watching me every time we kiss

Ah, so it is!

Some days are magnificent until evening

On such a day, there, in the eye of an early evening star, shimmers another life that someday you will have to live

NOTES

Page 45, 武川, Administrative region(縣) located in Hohhot(呼和浩特), Inner Mongolia(內蒙古自治區), China.

[2] Page 46, "Nanman" (南蠻) refers to the indigenous peoples who lived in the southern regions of ancient China. It literally means "southern barbarians" or "southern savages" in Chinese.

[3] Page 47, When Hamkyong Province is militarily divided, with Macheonryong set as boundaries, the north is called Pukkwan, south Namkwan.

[4] A district in Jeongseon, Gangwon-do.

[5] A Cuban Spanish-language radio station established by Ernesto Che Guevara in 1958.

ABOUT THE AUTHOR

Pak Jeong-de is the author of several notable works including Fragments (1997), In the *Gyeong-eyolbiyeol-do of My Youth*, *Snow Still Falls like Music* (2002), *Amur Guitar* (2004), *Chemical Origin of Love and Fever* (2007), *Distance of All Possibility* (2011), *Job That Is Called Life* (2011), *Hail, Che Guevara!* (2014), *From Her to Eternity* (2016), *Slavic Love* (2007), *Map of the French Orphan* (2019), *Short Stories* (2020), *Journey of Life*, *Comfort from Others* (2021), *La Rue du Flocon de Neige, or The Art of the Snowflake* (2021), and *Words of a Barbarian Traveling Through the Snow* (2023). Pak is the recipient of the 14th Kim Dal-jin Literature Prize, the 19th Sowol Poetry Prize, and the 22nd Daesan Literature Award. He is currently involved in the "Ezure Arcade Project" and is a member of the Sugarless Cigarette Club and the International Poetry Radical Barbarians' Band.

ABOUT THE TRANSLATORS

Eun-Mi Yang is a poet with five books, including poetry collections and anthologies, and has translated dozens of works, including the book *The Two Koreas*. She studied creative writing at the University of Edinburgh, where she won the Grierson Verse Prize. One of her poems was nominated for the 2015 Best of the Net Awards in the USA, and her translations have been featured in *Asymptote*, the *Guardian*, and more. She won the Modern Literature Translation Award from *The Korea Times* and currently teaches Creative Writing at Shilla University.

Ed Bok Lee is the author of three books, including *Whorled* and *Mitochondrial Night*, as well as plays, essays, and other fabulisms. Lee's poetry has been translated into French, Italian, Spanish, Korean, and Chinese. Book awards include an American Book Award, an Asian American Book Award (Members' Choice Award), a Minnesota Book Award, and a PEN/Open Book Award, among other honors. As a translator, he has worked from Russian and Korean, and is a recipient of *The Korea Times'* Modern Korean Literature Translation Award. Lee attended kindergarten in Seoul, and studied and worked variously while attending university (at Minnesota, Yonsei (Seoul), Al-Farabi Kazakh National (Almaty), Indiana, Berkeley, and Brown). With a background in local journalism and political theater, he teaches at Metro State University in Minneapolis/St. Paul, MN.

ABOUT THE SERIES

The Moon Country Korean Poetry Series publishes new English translations of contemporary Korean poetry by both mid-career and up-and-coming poets who debuted after the IMF crisis. By introducing work which comes out of our shared milieu, this series not only aims to widen the field of contemporary Korean poetry available in English translation, but also to challenge orientalist, neo-colonial, and national literature discourses. Our hope is that readers will inhabit these books as bodies of experience rather than view them as objects of knowledge, that they will allow themselves to be altered by them, and emerge from the page with eyes that seem to see "a world that belongs to another star."

*From the poem "Moon Country Mischief" by Kim Soo-young